A Walk in
Maggie's
Shoes

Maggie Payne

*Dedicated to my family and friends who have
been the driving force behind this book.*

A Walk in Maggie's Shoes

Maggie Payne

BREWIN BOOKS

First published by
Brewin Books Ltd, 19 Enfield Ind. Estate,
Redditch, Worcestershire B97 6BY in 2020
www.brewinbooks.com

ISBN: 978-1-85858-719-6

A Cataloguing in Publication Record
for this title is available from the British Library.

Typeset in Haarlemmer MT Std
Printed in Great Britain by
Hobbs The Printers Ltd.

CONTENTS

Chapter 1

ALL CHANGE

It's time I wrote about my life in Alcester, the good times and the bad, the scrapes I got into and the free spirit I was – which I am sure we all were at some point in our lives. These were the best years of my life and some of the situations I found myself in!

Meandering around the town today I walk by places to remind myself of the beauty of Alcester. Meeting Lane – gosh how it has changed, where the old bakery used to be all those years ago, I believe it closed in the 1950s. Following that a café opened with a juke box, something the local Teddy boys loved. On a Sunday morning after Sunday School and chapel I would remind myself that my mother warned me not to go in there but I couldn't help myself. Once I saw my younger brother inside, of course he didn't like seeing me in there and tried very hard to get rid of me, he said he would tell mother, so I said 'then she will also know you have been in here!' My friend and I would buy a bottle of Vimto and enjoy watching them all rocking and rolling. Now, from the late 60s to the present day, this building is a very smart white-painted house amongst the quaint cottages adorned with flowers in their window boxes.

There are many places I find in the town, and yes, though a small town it is very much like a village, where everyone knows everyone else. Within the quaint buildings are no end of coffee mornings and afternoon teas to visit. In the centre is the old Town Hall, looking just the same as it has always been.

Across the road in Henley Street is one of the oldest houses in Alcester, a lovely cottage with a long garden, it looks tiny. The other oldest house is at the top of Malt Mill Lane, known as The Malt House, probably dating from about 1500. How lovely to see so many black and white buildings, all of these cottages have retained their character, the residents have taken great pride in making them attractive with the hanging baskets and floral boxes hanging from their windows.

Walking to the alleyway on the left there is a tiny reception room open for anyone to sign a book and write down their thoughts on this beautiful complex, with a discreet donation box on the table. This little room was known as Uncle Tom's Cabin as you would often find Tom Marshall sat in there amusing those who called in.

Following the path there are other newly built bungalows leading down to a modern Community Hall right by the river. It is here I meet two gentlemen sat in light garden chairs enjoying the sun. Arthur and Geoff – what a lovely sight, both with their straw hats on enjoying a glass of malt. Geoff wanders off for a few minutes, returning with a large glass of gin and tonic for me! What bliss to sit with these two lovely gentlemen as they tell me their stories and watch the fish float by, across the river, sitting quietly on a branch is a kingfisher.

Time flies by and I thank the two gents for their lovely company and move on to the High Street walking through what is locally known as a 'Tury'. There are a few in Alcester, all short cuts to main roads. Walking through you can smell the delicious aroma of food cooking coming from The Royal Oak. I often meet my good friend Yvonne outside the Post Office and we go into the pub for lunch and catch up, I could do with something to eat to soak up the gin! The atmosphere is always so very different at lunchtimes, tourists walk in and eavesdropping we can tell they will be back again to visit our lovely little town.

Chapter 2

INCIDENTS AND MISHAPS IN CHURCHES: THE BAPTIST CHURCH

I fondly remember Alcester Baptist Church. Walking through the double doors how crisp and clean everything looked, especially during their annual Flower Festival. All the windows and tiny corners were filled with brightly coloured flowers, how wonderful it would be to be talented at flower arranging. I remember as a child seeing the 'open swimming pool' used for baptisms, now covered over. I was sent to the Baptist Church from the age of five to thirteen morning, noon and night!

They would occasionally have guest speakers and one Sunday morning, I guess I was about eleven years old, a new speaker arrived and announced his name. Immediately I knew this was a man my mother had talked about and he was a relative of ours. I plucked up the courage to announce myself to which he enquired how the family was? I replied they were very well and if he had time after the service my mother would love to see him. I ran all the way home after the service, excited to tell my mother we were going to have a visitor, the relative she had told me about. What did she do? Threw her arms up in the air and said 'that's all I want!'.

Apparently, he wasn't the best of relatives and was coming just as my mother was preparing Sunday lunch and my father would be coming home from the pub. I soon made myself scarce and as instructed took my father out in the back garden as this relative did not approve of alcohol at all. I quickly picked a garden fork up and gave it to my father, explaining he was not to go into the house yet. When the relative left he came out to the garden and mentioned how unusual to meet a man dressed so neatly whilst

Alcester Baptist Church in Victorian times.

gardening. My father said he was only ticking the earth over before Sunday lunch! Years went by and I had occasion to see this gentleman again but from a distance, I kept out of the way this time.

I often think of the hole in my knee caused when I was racing into the Baptist Church. I slipped and fell onto the jagged curb and cut my knee open. Despite a lovely lady trying to stop the bleeding in the Baptist kitchen, I needed to go to the local Doctor. Unfortunately, he was having an afternoon nap after his Sunday lunch so I had to go back the next day when he said my knee should have been stitched, my mother said 'it should have been but you had been on the whisky!' I ended up having some powder placed on it and bandages for what seemed ages, and having to miss my favourite lesson – physical education or PE.

Chapter 3

CHURCH OF ENGLAND: REVEREND EMRYS JONES!

Some years later I moved to St Nicholas Church. I have to admit this was after the Pastor's wife at the Baptist Church wanted me and a few others to be baptised.

She had invited us to her house for afternoon tea and then a trip to Ullenhall Church. None of us knew what this was for until we arrived there, where we were seated at the front. There in front of us was this open pool and straight away we knew why we had been invited. I personally felt, as a young teenager, I was being pushed into something and being controlled. I went home afterwards and told my mother of the experience, to which she said I must make my own mind up. So I decided to move over to St Nicholas Church, although I have very fond memories and still enjoy visiting the Baptist Church.

I decided to join the choir which was an experience, you get to see most of what's going on downstairs. I, along with my friend Esme, regularly went to Evensong and at the time I thought it a little boring, but now it all comes back to me the Psalms, Magnificat and Nunc Dimittis, not forgetting the seven-fold Amen at the end. Every Sunday we would sing an anthem before the sermon.

This was in the time of Reverend Emrys Jones, a conventional man who fitted in well with what was a small town then. All was going fine until my friend Esme nudged me and said 'don't move, my contact lens has come out and fallen on the floor'. This was while I was stood right next to Reverend Emrys Jones during the singing of *Immortal, Invisible, God Only Wise*. What was I to do? I couldn't stand up for the entire service! Occasionally the Reverend Emrys Jones would look down to the congregation so I discreetly bobbed down on the floor looking for this contact lens and luck was on my side as I saw this tiny tear drop glistening at me. The service carried on and Esme was able to guess the words of the hymns without her contact lens, placing it back in her eye after!

Another time of hilarity, I was sat next to my dear friend Betty, again in the choir. On this particular evening there was quite a big Civic service going on and we all stood up as the procession wove round the church with the acolytes on either side of the gentleman carrying the cross, followed by the flag bearer. All of a sudden a loud crashing sound rang through the church as the poor flag bearer did not see the chandelier and both the flag and the chandelier were swinging to the beat of the music. We stifled a giggle knowing the congregation could see us and that would never do. Following that, the sermon went on a little longer than anticipated and I quietly sat chewing the mint polos the choir always had hidden, when I caught sight of a very smart, quaint looking lady, sitting very stiffly but moving her head from side to side. This fascinated me, so I whispered to Betty 'see the lady with lovely curly hair? She reminds me of Coppelia from the ballet'. Well, I thought Betty was going to collapse with laughter! She then set me off, tears ran down our faces. We had to face the altar so the congregation could not see us but found out after they knew something had sparked us off as our shoulders were moving up and down!

Chapter 4

ME AND VICARS

What is it with me and vicars? It always seemed to be me causing mayhem. The Reverend Arthur Stally soon joined our church, he was a lively man with a lovely modern family and a beautiful large white dog. He accepted people's little ways and never took offence when Owen Evans would quietly walk out during the second hymn, knowing the sermon was about to start. Owen would stand outside in the porch, light his cigarette up, walk around the garden and go back in when he heard the singing of the next hymn.

Seated next to the Rev Stally and in front of the men in the choir singing Tenor and Alto, it was easy to pass the mint polos round to the vicar and to the men making sure the ladies had theirs first! Depending how long the sermon was from visiting vicars, one packet was never enough. If Reverend Stally took the sermon he would often say the sermon will be meaningful but short as *The Onedin Line* is on at 7.30!

One particular summer it was very hot. The Rev Stally kindly gave the choir permission to wear what they liked to ease the burden of the heavy robes being so uncomfortable. Myself and a few others wore our shorts knowing the congregation would not see. Not so! We came to the end of the service, the choir bowed to the altar and turned to process down the church. Guess whose robe got caught on something? There were my legs for all the world to see. Some smiled as I passed them, some, a few little old ladies, frowned in disgust!

We then had another service where a visiting clergyman from higher up came. During the service he stood in front of one of the lit candles and I could smell smoke so I glanced to the side of me and the vicar's surplice was about to go up in flames. I quickly brushed him down, what he was thinking I don't know, but I just got an evil glare. Not so much as a thank you!

When Alcester held its first Roman Market Day where the town all dressed appropriately, Reverend Stally was seen in a magnificent outfit which resembled something we had all seen regularly in our church life!

Christmas is always special in any church, with many services held. On Christmas Eve, the tradition was for myself and my friend Esme to go out and have a quiet drink or two, then go to Midnight Mass. One particular Christmas Eve there was kind of a light drizzle so we needed our umbrellas as we walked to The Bear pub in the High Street. We must have been sat in there for quite a long time watching the lovely log fire burning, oblivious to what was going on outside. At 10.30pm we thought we should make a move and go to church. On entering the High Street little did we know we had had heavy snow, what a shock! Of course, most of us know when you have been sat in a warm room of any kind and go outside into the cold after drinking you don't feel so clever. Esme and I both decided now was not the time to go straight into church so we would walk around the town for a while first and get our acts together, feeling very uncertain of ourselves at the time. I mentioned to Esme, I hoped we could get through the service, when a voice behind us said 'I'm sure you will girls, the water tap is in the vestry should you need it beforehand'. It was the Rev Stally!

Yes, we made it to church and did not let ourselves down but unfortunately as we were singing *The First Noel* down went our other friend sitting opposite us. There was no time to give, what choir members know as sign language, so the gents picked her up and carried her out. We did not see her again until the following Sunday when she sang like an angel.

Another lovely Christmas tradition was when the choir were invited to Carol sing at various houses. Mrs Pamela Norman made the best mulled wine ever, I'm not sure what was in it but it certainly made you sing better. Then onto Mike and Caroline Newey's house which can only be described as a Christmas card scene with decorations adorning the bannisters and the choir standing on each winding step as all their guests looked on dressed in the festive spirit. We ended up at The Rectory where we were invited in by

Ann, the Reverend Stally's wife, to see their new baby Boudicca. They had the biggest decorated Christmas Tree I had ever seen and there was this tiny baby waiting to greet the world. By now mince pies and hot punch were most welcome.

During one summer Reverend Stally acquired a massive steam engine which was parked in the driveway of Butter Street and the Rectory. It wasn't known why he had bought it at the time, however, it was announced in church if anyone would like to polish it up, they were most welcome. I quite liked the idea so with some friends we climbed up and set to polishing and cleaning. The following summer there was a Donkey Derby held in the grounds of Ragley Hall and many people enjoyed picnics with their families. There in all its glory was the steam engine I and a few friends had lovingly looked after. The donkey race was hilarious! Yes, even Reverend Stally was in it and the sun shone down on a perfect day for everyone.

Chapter 5

CANON DAVID CAPRON

After some years Canon David Capron came along, again with a young family. Times were changing and it was okay to call him David, although one lady insisted on calling him Father, as at times David would introduce incense and the said lady thought it very fitting. Now a lot of people would cough and splutter and did not like the smell but I have to admit I loved it! When the time came to use it, David would announce to the choir to let them know what to expect. Some would quietly mutter under their breath. As for me I asked when he swished it across the choir to give me a double dose as I loved the smell.

Eric, my husband, was usually the first to arrive at church ready to ring the bells. He was often seen beforehand, placing the cross and the candles in the right position on the altar. It was an obsession he had.

David and his wife Hilary had three boys, all community minded and could be seen doing odd jobs around the town, especially helping Alcester in Bloom. All the boys helped with lifting the hanging baskets onto the poles, adorning the streets in the summer. David was one for socialising. Often, he would have a get together in his house, on reaching his door there was always a welcome and a whisper of 'your gin's in the kitchen'! I told the other guests it was sparkling water while other guests drank red wine, but I'm sure they knew. David would creep out with Eric and they would light their pipes, while Hilary and I could catch up without any interruption.

Eric was often seen gardening around the church. If he wasn't at the front of the church green, he could be seen enjoying his pipe along with Canon Capron on the seat at the back of the church.

One evening, it was time for confirmation candidates. Eric and I, along with friends Betty and Norman were invited to three young people's house after the service. We tried to work out a route to follow as we would be walking. We got to the first house and as many times when we were out, we spilt up and mixed with others. Betty had mentioned she would need the Ladies room as it had been a long night, I suggested she ask at the house and left it at that. We then went onto another house but then realised time was getting on and maybe the Capron family (the last house to visit) had gone to bed. Not so, we walked to the house to see if it was in darkness and there were the three boys waiting for us in the window. Betty then announced again about the Ladies room, as she hadn't asked at the previous house, unbelievable! In we go and end the night with good company. Leaving quite late, Betty was walking extremely quickly. I said to slow down but it was too late. All I'm saying is a beautiful bottle green silk dress was ruined! We reached home where the dress was taken off and Betty went home in my husband's large jumper and a bath towel wrapped round her. Again, we laughed until we cried.

There were so many good times with Betty, especially New Year's Eve, when she and her husband Norman would always walk to our house due to the consumption of drink during the night. We had a lovely evening with neighbours popping in around midnight after they had danced the Conga around the road. On leaving in the early hours of the morning, Betty and Norman had to walk home. One year, little did we realise snow had fallen and the ice was treacherous. However, they both insisted they would 'slide' home on the promise they would ring me when they got there. This they did and gave me a report on how they got home with no shoes on as it was too dangerous. It doesn't bear thinking about!

Always trying to make birthdays special, myself and Betty decided to dress up and do a Kissogram for Canon David Capron. Dressed in just white shirts, black dickie bows and fishnet tights we decided to give him a call armed with a tray of goodies and a cake. Did I mention I wrote an ode for him? I had warned Hilary, his wife, not to say a word that we would be calling round.

Off we went after changing our clothes in the Lady Chapel in the church, walking down the narrow alleyway to his house and knocking on the door. He answered looking very surprised, as I read out a risky poem on his doorstep. Little did we know his mother was stood behind the door! What must she have thought, but she did appear after and said 'how wonderful'. I can tell you I breathed a sigh of relief! We were invited in, the cake was cut and the medication came out (G&T) and it turned out a frolicking good night!

I well remember when mobile phones came out. I had put mine in my handbag in the vestry while the service carried on. Just as Canon David was about to give the sermon what did I hear? My mobile ringing to the tune of the *Can Can*! I just sat

Canon David Capron outside St Nicholas Church, Alcester.

innocently and pretended it belonged to someone else. Eric sat behind me in the choir and I heard him mutter 'she's done it again' in a disgruntled voice! The following week Canon Capron announced if anyone had a mobile phone could they please turn it off. The service was just about to start and guess who's mobile went off? Not mine this time, but his!

Canon Capron had a modern approach to meeting people. The local pub was the venue and many marriages and christenings were arranged there. The other option was to see him sat on the bench outside the church chatting to the community.

Chapter 6

OTHER CHURCHES

I once had cause to visit another church out of town. Such a lovely big building, but a very hot day. By the time the service finished I was wilting and no longer could I stand wearing the hold ups with elastic at the top, they were so uncomfortable. Thankfully I was one of the last to leave the church, I asked my friend Mike to stand in front of me but not to turn around. This he did so I slipped the hold ups off and put them in my handbag, I then walked out feeling much better. I'm sure the Lord understands me and my ways!

I actually liked visiting many different churches during one special year, the Sikh temple was fascinating but sitting cross legged for three hours was a bit much for me, although the people were all very welcoming. The temple was beautifully decorated and we were asked to take our shoes off and put headscarves on to cover our hair. No point in having a fancy hairstyle as no one could see it, but we always respected other church's traditions. The men sat on one side and the ladies on the other. The regular older generation had got it right, managing to sit with their backs against the radiators to keep nice and warm.

I had never been to a Quaker Meeting before but found it extremely meditational. Sat in a small room with just the clock to look at, no hymns, just a few readings. We were asked to just sit quietly with our own thoughts. At the time both my husband and I were just getting over the flu so agreed it would be best to sit at the back for fear of coughing. Gosh! For that one hour we got through a packet of eucalyptus sweets just in case we both had coughing fits. After we were taken out into a back garden, considering it was on a busy road, you could not hear a sound. So peaceful.

I'm thinking it was a church in Rugby we attended, but I'm not sure. How different the layout was, very cleverly done so that the vicar stood in the middle on a rostrum and the chairs were in a circle around him, making it possible for him to speak to everybody and not so boring for him having to stand and look at everybody in front.

Alcester held a Civic Service one year where I was asked, along with my husband, to sit in the front pew by a pillar thankfully to the side of the church. Next to me was The Lord Lieutenant, Tim Cox, he was an absolutely lovely gent. His costume was very elegant with his sword strapped to his side, which he then carefully took out and laid on the rim of the front pew. Now, your thoughts were like mine, I must be careful not to knock it off onto the tiled floor during the service! Nothing went to plan. We had just finished singing a hymn and were about to sit down, when who totally forgot the sword was there? My little finger just tipped the sword which was about to drop on the floor when thankfully both our reflexes moved at the same time and our hands automatically stretched out and caught the sword. I smiled to myself as it very much looked like a sketch from *Morecambe and Wise* with them doing a song and dance act!

I had cause to go to a funeral at the local Catholic Church. My neighbours had the job of organising their friend Byron's funeral as under very sad circumstances he had passed away on the plane coming over to visit. There were just five of us there to give support. I was invited back to the burial where the catholic priest finalised the service. Slightly different to the C of E, towards the end the priest sprinkled the coffin with holy water and then it was passed round. Not being used to this I thought I would copy what the others were doing. When we returned home my neighbour said 'Margaret, what on earth were you doing with the holy water?' I asked 'why?' His reply was 'you looked as if you were sprinkling vinegar on fish and chips!' Another lesson learnt!

I have not mentioned the local Methodist Church. My mother was not a Methodist, but she always took me to the Harvest Festival Service in Priory Road as a child. What an array of fruit and veg, all neatly arranged in a pattern, I can see it now so distinctly and I remember the smell inside the

On the far left the original Methodist Church, Priory Road, Alcester.
The building was demolished in 1966 and a replacement constructed.

tiny church. That was the only church my mother went to for Harvest Festival. Now very much modernised with a lovely front garden and used for many different things.

Chapter 7

MOVING ON TO MY YOUTH!

Well the time had come for serious thinking about boyfriends. Where to start?

I was working in a shop on the High Street when along came a new member of staff, a very nice man, everyone loved his humour but we were all intrigued. After a while the other girls working in the shop bet me money that I could not go out with him within the week. Each week day passed and we walked home together until the last day came, we chatted and he asked what was I doing that weekend? I said I hoped to go to the cinema but my friend had let me down so I was quite disappointed. SUCCESS! He then said he would like to go so should we go together? I knew then I would be picking up a tidy sum of money and had won the bet. The relationship lasted almost two years but it turned out, although he was a lovely man, I was too young to settle down and so a sad end came but the right decision.

Who would believe the church kept cropping up in my life? One lovely gentleman joined the church choir while he was staying with friends. A nice gentleman who just wanted company for the few days or weeks he was there. I had no complaints about him at all but we both knew he would be gone soon and we had a great time socialising. We said we would keep in touch which we did for a while but then it dwindled out and that was that.

I was going out with my friend Katy and was fascinated visiting the different pubs and meeting the different clientele. At the time The Royal Oak pub was owned by Mrs Jobson, running the pub on her own she certainly knew what the customers wanted and was very able to throw someone out if they misbehaved. She could be seen every morning with the door wide open sweeping the path. After this lady retired the pub had new owners and was fully refurbished. What a difference it made to the town! Residents and tourists poured in especially during the hot summer months.

I was with my friend Katy sat in The Bear public house having a nice quiet drink one evening when we both noticed two males were looking across. Over they came, made polite conversation and we found we all had the same interests but I noted the one I was talking to had said he preferred ladies not to drink alcohol! What was I to do? I liked him very much but whenever drinks were ordered I had an orange juice and then the inevitable happened. It was almost closing time at The Bear and my friend being new to the town asked what I would like to do? I did know there was a karaoke evening at the Red Horse Hotel, he seemed to like the sound of this so off we went.

The Landlord and his wife, Gertie and Tom, were very pleased to see us. As we walked upstairs, we could hear the sound of music, I opened the door and who should be in there but my brother Norman and his wife Maxine. How lovely to meet up! We did the introductions and then my new friend asked what I would like to drink? He went to get the drinks while my

The Bear, High Street, Alcester.

brother asked 'what on earth are you drinking orange juice for?' I said, 'to be honest, my new friend does not agree with ladies drinking alcohol, he's a lovely man but I can't drink any more orange juice tonight and he doesn't seem to approve of the singing'. My brother gave me a look of what can only be surmised as 'this is not you'!

Deep down, as the minutes went by, I was not enjoying myself so I asked my brother if I feigned a headache would he take my friend to the bus stop (as the other two friends had gone elsewhere). Yes, it sounds underhand but sometimes needs must. There I sat with a look of woe on my face and the plan went perfectly, off went my brother and took my friend to the nearest bus stop. Now, I could relax.

Sadly, or happily depending which way you look at it, I was sat in pleasant company all round. An old friend of mine started singing Sonny and Cher's song *I Got You Babe*, he was trying to get up on the table so I gave him a little help, wherein he pulled me onto the table as well, so we ended up singing the song together. Everything was very harmless and good fun.

Time to go home, as to what time it was, I had no idea. My brother Norman and his wife drove home and a good neighbour of mine said we could walk home together. This was fine but just before home was a small wood and I was asked if I wanted to stop for a while in there! My reply was 'I can't believe you just said that! Your wife is a very good friend of mine and there's no way I'm going anywhere with you'. He apologised so I knew he had got the message! We stayed friends and nothing was ever mentioned again.

Chapter 8

THE ERRORS OF MY WAYS!

I worked in the local fruit and veg shop for a while and quite a few local gentlemen were regulars. My then boss said I got on 'too well' with them, I took this as a compliment! One such gentleman was a farmer type. Every day he would come into the fruit and veg shop and stare at me. My boss said it wouldn't be long before he asked me out. The day came and yes, he did, so I got into his car and asked where he lived, the reply was 'in the woods with my two Alsatian dogs'! Again, I'm sorry to say I feigned a headache and he took me home after one drink at a country pub. I was in the house by 9.30pm, I rushed in, leant against the door and said 'I have just been saved'. Wherein my mother said 'that serves you right my girl, philandering with too many men'!

It did teach me a lesson at the time but sadly it never lasted long. Following that there was a dance that weekend at the local Greig Memorial Hall. My boss had asked 'who is your target for this weekend?' My thoughts were 'who knows'! However, off I went with my friend Esme. We always shared the buying of the drinks and when it was my turn to buy, off I went to the bar, as I went to pay I knocked a gentleman's drink over! I was so apologetic and embarrassed and he was very nice and said not to worry, we will have a dance to put things right. This we did and as I passed my boss dancing, he looked at me and just said 'unbelievable'! I innocently said to my boss the next morning 'it just happened'!

Again, it was a nine-minute wonder as we had nothing in common except for dancing. Meanwhile his friend, an Italian, was far more interesting and fun loving. The inevitable happened, I ended up seeing him for several months. I travelled to his home town on the train for the weekend and met his lovely family. That evening it was suggested we went to a local Disco. Everything was going so well, such friendly people except for one cocky youth who continuously was interrupting and making innuendos towards me. He was asked politely to move away but no, he insisted on staying and thought he could win me over. Before I could say anything, I turned around and the cocky youth was on the floor. My then boyfriend's brother was apparently a boxer and had knocked him out! Within minutes the youth was carried out into the streets and no more was said.

Needless to say, this romance fizzled out. You can always tell, when the date nights start dwindling down. It turned out this boyfriend had found another girl, I was devastated but hey ho, life goes on. I do recollect one man I went out with who, when I asked his surname, said it was 'Woolhead'. Immediately I knew that was only going to be a one-night stand. I might be a dumb blonde but not that dumb. He went out the door the same night.

Then a very nice young man moved into Alcester. I felt like my luck had turned! We would walk for miles and often end up in the local Grammar School field to just chat about our likes and dislikes. Sadly, this will sound odd, but he was far too nice for me, he deserved someone better. Gifts, flowers, perfume. I could not be bought!

Well, I should have mentioned my good friend Esme and I had a pact. When either of us were at a loose end we would meet up if there was no boyfriend in tow. It worked out well for both of us. Many evenings after church we were invited, along with different choir members, back to Vic Butler's house a couple of miles away. His mother kindly did food and drink was plentiful. Music played in the background and there was a lovely atmosphere.

I would meet a group of friends during the summer, all motorbike addicts, but extremely friendly. It wasn't long before I went out with one of them. I distinctly remember going to Coventry to see The Bees motorbike racing. Not a place I would go to again! The smell and the dust made me feel sick and when I needed the ladies loo, off I went and sadly walked into the gents by mistake. The notices said 'Colts' on one door and 'Fillies' on the other. Yes, I went in the wrong one, thankfully the gents did not see me!

It was nearing winter and the same person I was going out with decided we would go to Stratford cinema, I couldn't wait to get on the back of his bike again. On leaving the cinema the snow was coming down really heavily, guess who had no helmet on? Coming down Red Hill was wonderful, but when I got home I can only describe my head as looking like one of the Queen's soldier's bearskin hats, only pure white. What a sight I looked!

Then there was Irish Patrick. Half the time I couldn't understand what he said and he only lasted a week because he was doing my head in talking nonstop about how he was going to change the world!

I really think over the years I have met many kinds of people but again as my good friend says they are 'all part of life's rich tapestry'!

Chapter 9

THE OVER FRIENDLY MAGGIE

I truly believe whoever we are, male or female, we all get into scrapes in our teenage years.

One such time I was invited out to a darts match. Whoever the team was, they needed one more player as one member had not turned up. They asked me but I declined saying I was rubbish at darts. Pressure was put on me, so I gave in! The first dart landed on the floor, then the second dart went into the open fire below and the third landed in a gentleman's pint of beer. How awful did I feel? I was most apologetic and the gentleman was very kind and insisted instead of me buying him a pint he bought me a drink.

I wasn't asked to continue in the matches but the said gentleman was being very friendly. For several weeks after I would go and watch the darts and we sat and chatted with friends until one evening in walked my gentleman friend with a lady. Yes, you have guessed, it was his wife. There was no hint of a smile not even an 'hello'. My guess is he had been rumbled. Several times after he appeared in the local High Street waiting for me to finish work. Instinct told me to ignore him, after a few weeks he gave up and I never went to the dart matches again. I think they call it 'saved by the bell'!

Chapter 10

CARNIVALS AND LONG HOT SUMMERS

One of the highlights of the year was the many weeks of preparing for the carnivals. One particular year I decided, as I was in the junior drama group, we would do Robin Hood and His Merry Men. So many tree branches! All the children were dressed in their green outfits and looked lovely. They were all very excited to be riding on a lorry dressed up. It was a boiling hot day and yes, you might guess what happened, everything wilted but we did have a lot of fun that day.

Our best ever float was The Hawaii Girls with lots of coloured rosettes made into garlands to cover the lorry. Raffia skirts were made with all the girls wearing Bloomfield bras from Woolworths, for those that remember they were black with dainty flowers on. Garlands were strewn round our necks and a tape played Hawaiian music. Try dancing and swaying on a lorry with no sides on! Around the town we went, ending up at the renowned Greig Memorial Hall grounds where there was the summer fete with Alcester Victoria Silver Band in attendance. We won the trophy and also that year did the same at Bidford and Redditch.

In the 60s we did not have the Food Festivals, the Annual Street Markets, the Duck Races, the Flower Festivals, the Street parties and all the many fund-raising events that go on now. Instead it was Carnivals, Discos and just enjoying the era of bright lights, bright clothes and very carefree days.

Us girls could not wait for the weekend when we would catch the bus to Birmingham and walk round all the boutiques, always coming home with the latest fashions. The dresses were psychedelic, full of bright colours, frills round the neck and arms, very feminine. Chokers were worn around the neck and gold buckled belts round the waist. Shoes had moved from stilettos to chunky heels. Hairstyles were either very short or bouffant and back-combed to a bee hive effect. Shopping bags were called Gondola baskets, everyone seemed to have one even though they ripped your tights!

As for the boys, can you imagine they wore all colours of the rainbow for trousers and shirts. Hair was long, the more they had the better they looked. Now, times have changed again, the men can't wait to shave their hair off. Shoes were also chunky, moving from the winkle pickers. Motorbikes and Vespa Scooters were all the rage. I remember my youngest brother having a scooter and coming off it in an accident. He ended up with a skin graft taken from his rear end to put on his arm. It's strange how times change and we do not see many scooters about now.

I often used to spend Saturday afternoons at Exhall and Wixford cricket ground, helping the ladies with the teas. I never did understand the game but it was good fun watching the men playing the game so seriously.

Chapter 11

MOVING TO THE FINAL GENTLEMAN

I do remember going out with a chef who worked locally. My mother disapproved as she said his socks looked thin! What was that all about? However, it was nearing Christmas and I had bought a large box of assorted Brut men's accessories for him. The inevitable happened, the chef moved on and I was left with this wonderful present (I should mention that before agreeing to see the chef I had my eye on Eric Payne!). I couldn't wait for Evensong on Sunday nights, Eric and I would be eyeing each other up across the choir stalls… if the hymn seemed appropriate, we would both look across at each other with just a hint of interest. Reverend Stally noticed and would go home and tell his wife Ann that he was aware something was going on!

There was the usual Christmas dance in the local Town Hall at the time. Again, with my friend Esme, we enjoyed the night but Mr Eric Payne was there and was very stubborn, pretending he hadn't noticed me until the last dance and then he asked me to do the last waltz with him. I was in my element especially when he said he would walk me home! I invited him in for coffee and yes, he agreed to come in, I thought to myself I'm half way there. We were very romantic until I heard the bang on the bedroom floor. It was my mother! Poor Eric said it was late and he should go. I went upstairs to hear my mother chastising me and saying 'Esme's mother will be worried to death keeping her out this late at night' to which I replied it was not Esme downstairs it was Eric Payne. After I announced this she put her bedroom light on and said 'my God, you keep in with him my girl he comes from good stock'!

What did I do? Only visited his home on Christmas morning with the said Brut present which was meant for the chef! Obviously, it was a shock to his system to see me in his living room. The poor man felt obliged to give me a lift home. Of course, I did not refuse. From then onwards we saw each other every night for four years except for when work took him abroad for one week.

Yes, I had a good innings, far more than I have written about but everyone was an experience! As many of you might think, you just know when the right one comes along. It was plain to see I was very blessed with Eric. My mother had found a list in my bedroom of boys I had been out with, I had put a tick by the good ones and a cross by the not so good. She announced 'if I were you, my girl, I would burn that book', for once I did as she said! It was obvious Eric was in her good books, every Saturday night no matter how late we were coming in, she would make cheese on toast for him. None for me!

Eric was a gentleman in every way, he could be serious but his humour was something else. He never did ask me to marry him, we just drifted into it! However, he did ask for my mother's permission to which she replied 'that's the best news I've heard yet Eric, you will make a better job than I did. The very best of luck, take her with my blessing!'

At times we seemed a little like Morecambe and Wise. Eric with his quips, especially when meeting new people. He would introduce me and (I smile as I write this) he would say 'this is my wife Maggie… try not to laugh at her'. Many wives would take offence, but not me, I actually enjoyed wondering what he was going to come out with next and I'm sure the recipients knew that.

Chapter 12

SCHOOL HOUSE

The Reverend Arthur Stally said he was so fed up with seeing us not married after four years, so we were to sort ourselves out. He offered us rented accommodation in School Road and said it used to be the Curate's house but was empty and would need doing up. Off we went to look at it and as we walked in through the door there was a long tiled mosaic hallway but there was no electric or lighting so we could see no more. We both knew straight away there was something about the place, it had a lovely feel about it.

On returning in the daylight, oh my goodness what a shock! Still ideal, but the curate had not had the money to keep it as it should have been. The long lounge had an historic fireplace and mantlepiece, the dining room was just dilapidated, the kitchen with the old-fashioned Rayburn stove was lovely but what a state it was in! There was an old-fashioned pantry with plenty of shelves and underneath the stairs was a very useful hidey hole. Walking up the stairs, with a very high ceiling, we wondered who would do the job of decorating? Upstairs was very cold looking, three bedrooms with old-fashioned iron fireplaces. The one joy was the bathroom, it had been converted from a bedroom and was huge! Previous to the curate living there it had been used for the Headmasters of the school next door for many years. Mr Collins, Mr Jenkins and Mr Wilson had all used it as a lovely family home.

We first looked at the house on our annual Mop night in Alcester 1972 and then the rush was on to get everything sorted before we were married. Why we decided the date of early December I will never know as it took 10 weeks to convert each room, plus decorating the very tall stairway. My

School House.

brothers Stan and David took charge and banned us from going! We sneaked a look when they had gone and found the fireplace was ripped out and a lovely Cotswold stone fireplace put in with two alcoves either side. The dining room and lounge had been painted and freshly wallpapered, the kitchen walls which originally looked like painted brick walls had all been chipped off, plastered and painted.

Eric and I had great joy in literally scrubbing the Rayburn down to its original state which proved to be a Godsend in the winter, warming the whole house through and its oven cooked meals were perfect. My greatest joy was having the old-fashioned walk-in pantry with lovely long shelves for all the separate boxes and tins of food. Because the house was in such a state, the rent was dirt cheap but we were told if the school closed then we would have to move as it was attached and owned by the Marquis of Hertford.

The day came when all was perfect in the house and the wedding was to take place. I did not see Eric until reaching the top of aisle, I looked down and there by my feet was a wire, I suddenly realised the service was being recorded. It turned out that one of the bell ringers, Charles, had thought of the very kind gesture of recording everything but he had forgotten to plug the wire in! Poor Eric, a very strong singer, was shaking and I could just about hear him. I was shocked! Eric was the one who I was relying on to get me through this very serious ceremony.

Reverend Stally made an announcement, which at the time neither I nor Eric knew what he was talking about, but it seemed all the guests did as it caused a lot of laughter. Apparently my brothers had climbed onto the chimneys of our house and placed two large wooden cartoons, one was a stork carrying a baby and the other was a farmer with a shotgun pointing at the stork! Nobody mentioned it at the wedding reception but on the way to our honeymoon, passing the house, what a shock when we saw these two giant animations. They stayed up there for six months for all the world to see!

We chose to stay at The Lygon Arms in Broadway for our honeymoon as it was the middle of winter and coming up to Christmas. The room was beautiful with an old-fashioned latched door and on entering there was confetti strewn across the bed, a welcome drink for us both, chocolates and a lovely four-poster bed.

We were just about to eat our evening meal when I remembered I had left my handbag so went back up to fetch it. I looked in amazement as the beautiful cover over the bed now had no confetti on and was turned back, with fresh drinks on either side of the bed – how efficient were the staff there? On passing what seemed to be the Great Hall there was a Hunt Ball going on, I cannot publish what we saw!

This may sound very odd and boring to the reader but we knew an old Aunt lived a few miles away so we decided to visit her. She was a spinster and I well remember her crying when she saw us because we had bothered to visit her. We were so glad we went as she seemed to confide a lot in us and gave me a box of photos for safe keeping as she thought when she had left this earth they would be burnt. I still have them to this day after I photocopied them and gave them to the appropriate people. A strange honeymoon but we did remember it being a very cold weekend.

My plan was to return to our new home and impress Eric with my non-existent cooking skills. The first thing I did was to phone my mother and ask 'how do you cook a chicken?' After easy instructions, I set to peeling the potatoes, not a second had gone by when I noticed the water with the potatoes in had turned red. Yes, I had cut the end of my finger off! A trip to the Doctor's to have stitches in was a good start to married life and being told not to get the said finger wet! I returned a week later to have the stitches out dreading what the Doctor would say as it was obvious I had got the bandage and the finger wet. In I walked, he looked at my finger and said 'well done, you've managed to keep your finger dry!'

Chapter 13

FAMILY TRAUMA

Two years after our wedding along came our son Nick. Everything was rosy until just before his second birthday, a terrible hauntingly horrible thing happened. We visited my mother who had just said 'who wants a cup of tea?' Knowing Nick loved having Gran's tea out of his special cup (it hurts me to write this as I will carry it with me for the rest of my life) my mother, God Bless her, had 'warmed the pot'. Nick ran up to the small teapot and pulled it onto him. We all know things can happen in a flash. I cannot write about the trauma but he was rushed to Warwick hospital with burns to his chest, and arm.

We were interrogated as to how this accident had happened for over an hour, constantly repeating ourselves. We truly believed the only person who saved us was Reverend Arthur Stally. Strange as it sounds, one of the questions asked was 'did we belong to a church?' We then answered 'yes, St Nicholas in Alcester'. Within an hour the hospital staff changed their attitude and had rung the Reverend Arthur Stally to confirm what we had said. After that they were very compassionate towards us. I understood why we were interrogated as there were children in the same ward whose parents did not visit, it left me thinking.

Nick was in there for what seemed an eternity. I was very glad that my good friend Cynthia was also visiting her poorly father at the same hospital and was able to give me a lift in early in the morning. I sat with Nick until 7pm at night, with Eric coming straight from work, and also tried to amuse the other little children who rarely had visitors. So sad. They told me when Nick could walk and eat again properly, he could come home. Nick had forgotten how to walk. I did my utmost to get him to walk again, up and down the same ward. They gave him semolina… he ate the lot so I asked for more, they then said the next day he could come home.

Although after what seemed a duration we were back together as a family again it was another year before we could live a proper life again. It was nobody's fault, just an inquisitive child, but the memory sticks with you forever. You don't talk about it as it is too traumatic, but it's always there making you see danger far more than you ever did before.

Chapter 14

MARRIAGE DAYS AND MISHAPS

Eric tolerated me and my strange ways, then two years later on and I found I was pregnant again. Getting very bored at home I decided to do some gardening and remove a lot of stones with grass creeping through in between. It took me all day and I was so proud to announce to Eric 'guess what I've done today?' When I told him, his reply was 'very good, but you have dug the path up!' What can I say?

We had a Labrador named Sabre. The dog was getting old and was having trouble with his legs and walking was difficult. We were not able to get the dog in the car and thought his days were numbered. The vet kindly came out to see him and prescribed pills for arthritis in his legs. The next day off went Eric with the dog and I noticed, looking out of the window, the dog was almost running, Eric had a job to keep up with him! On returning we were both amazed and Eric thought the tablets too strong so we looked at the box and the instructions. He had given Sabre three pills at once instead of one pill three times a day, the dog must have thought it was his birthday! So, you see we were both as bad as each other. Eric was not that perfect.

Chapter 15

WILD LIFE

Although I love wildlife ask me to touch any and I would run away! Don't ask me why but the thought gives me the shudders.

My first encounter was using a Ewbank carpet sweeper. There I was going over the carpet and then it seemed stuck, I looked at the bottom of it and thought it had picked up a thick piece of wool. I went to pull it out, oh my Lord, it was only a mouse tail! No way could I touch it so I left it for Eric when he came home from work.

Next was on a lovely summer's day when at the time we had front windows opening out. I heard a fluttering and there was a blackbird flying around wondering where he was. Again, I had forty fits! What should I do? I ran over to our neighbour Eric Portman, explained my dilemma and he kindly came over and sorted it, getting the blackbird free. The furniture was all over the place but I didn't care.

Following that, this you may laugh at, there we were sitting in the front room but could see something flitting about. We had left the back door open and in came a bat! Again, up I shot off the sofa, daring myself to see how it could get out. Wait for it! I opened the back door wider and put the light on. Yes, you may be thinking the same as Eric, he asked why I had put the light on. I replied 'so he can see his way out'. Yes, I had forgotten bats are blind!

I'm not sure which is worse but this incident was last year in 2019. Nick, my son, went into the bathroom early one morning to get ready for work. He announced I might like to look behind the washing basket where I had also left a loo roll. Thinking he was having some sort of joke on me I went into the bathroom. There behind the laundry basket was a hedgehog! How on earth it got there and how long it had been there I honestly don't know. It had eaten some of the toilet roll! The wimp that I am, I immediately rang my friend Jean who seemed more interested in taking photos of it. I gave her an old towel and she gallantly picked it up and took it into the garden. The question is, to this day we don't know how it got there! What is it with me and wildlife?

Finally, we had the cats and pigeons. Oh My Lord, what a day that was! We owned two cats commonly known as Gin and Tonic. I had been to work and came home in the dinner hour, opened the kitchen door and what did I see? The floor carpet was covered in pigeon feathers. I was in shock! The biggest cat Gin was having a field day. A neighbour had brought home some dead pigeons in the back of his open truck. The said cat had found them and stolen them, bringing them home to us! It took me ages to get rid of all the feathers. Needless to say, after watching the cat having his adventure, I felt the need to go and speak to the neighbour who was very good about it and soon resolved the problem, much to the disgust of the cat.

An uninvited visitor.

Chapter 16

OUR FUNNY ASSORTED LIFE

Eric and I still carried on our social life and strange as it may seem although always together, we always tried to mix and mingle separately. I guess a few eyebrows were raised as both he and I would mix with the opposite sex and at times maybe not join up again until it was time to go home. It never changed in our 46 years of marriage. Why change the habit of a lifetime? We neither had time for jealousy. Eric went his way and I went mine but at the end of the day we were together. We enjoyed dances and friends' celebrations, often leaving a few minutes earlier saying 'we had to put the children to bed'. They were teenagers by then!

Eric always noticed people's clothes. One day I bought what I thought was a beautiful feminine pale pink trouser suit. Feeling really good in it, I came downstairs and said 'what do you think?' His reply was 'you look like a pink blancmange'! That was it the trouser suit came off and went to the charity shop, somebody had a bargain there.

On the fun side, one particular night we had gone to bed and just as I was dropping off to sleep Eric announced 'the bed's damp'! Now this was in the middle of summer and I knew very well it wasn't. However, I ignored him and three more times he muttered the word 'damp'. On the third time, despite trying to ignore him, I was trying so hard not to laugh. He then started laughing and despite me trying to close my ears to him we both ended up laughing until we cried. To anyone else it was nothing but neither of us could control ourselves so in the end I just said 'coffee' and we both went downstairs and pulled ourselves together. My last words were 'Eric the bed is not damp'.

One lovely summer's day we were invited to an evening wedding reception. Off we went, looking forward to a good time. The event we thought was at The Kings Court, near Alcester. We were greeted at the door and guided upstairs to where the beautiful bride and groom were. On opening the door and seeing the bride I quickly realised it was the wrong wedding! We discreetly made our way downstairs and remembered it was at The Moat House, next door!

The same thing happened with myself and Yvonne my very good friend. We were invited to a celebration party. Again, we got in the car and both said we were not sure where the venue was but pretty much had an idea. On reaching Studley Cricket Club we saw cars in the car park, walked in, went to the bar to order drinks, looked round and I happened to mention people were looking at us but we didn't recognise anyone! We asked the bar staff who said yes there was a function on in the next room. We moved to the said room, again not recognising anyone so thought to ask whose party it was. Yes, you have guessed, again we were at the wrong celebration party. Eventually we got to Joyce Mumford's celebration and had an excellent night. We were a little embarrassed about being late but all turned out okay!

Another time I heard of a lady I knew who had passed away and her funeral was to be the following week at the local St Joseph's Catholic Church. I felt I should attend as this lady, although not rich, gave me £5 every month towards Alcester in Bloom. Off I went only to be greeted by two gentleman who, before entering the church, asked me my name and was I representing anyone? This I gave, thinking how strange. I seated myself in the back seat of the church, looked around and saw ladies in fine hats and every seat being taken up. My thoughts were what a dark horse this deceased lady was! However, the service started and I looked at the service sheet only to find a lovely photo of a different lady. What a dilemma! I could not move, so thought it best to just sit through the service! Once home, I told Eric who just laughed and said 'one day you will get it right'!

Eric devoted his life, apart from council business, to St Nicholas Church Garden, the choir and bellringing for 60 years. He could often be seen repairing things in the church.

During the Christmas week, the Alcester Town Band would come and play Carols under the lamplight and then come in and have some sort of Christmas food. Christmas was always a routine. We would go to Midnight Mass on Christmas Eve. The following morning, nothing was more important to Eric than singing in the choir and ringing the church bells. He would then take an elderly friend to her family in Studley and then come home to carve the turkey. We would have a very relaxing afternoon but then early evening he would fetch our friend back from Studley and be able to sit and have a drink. New Year's Eve, again was different. Eric would ring the New Year in, followed by the refreshment of mince pies etc and whisky or whatever was on the bell ringers table. When he eventually came home, there would already be some sort of party going on in the house.

We enjoyed giving the occasional 'get together' with friends for certain occasions.

Eric loved being in the church garden working, many times forgetting the time! I had my contacts to find him if he was late coming home, the

Left to right: Stephen, Mark and Eric mending the church tiles.

main one was Mrs Jean James. I would ring her up and ask if she had seen him, knowing full well he had stopped working for the night and was sat having a malt whisky with her. Often, she would reply 'I think he is on his way home now'!

Eric was committed to the church and the community, it was an understanding we had if he was late for meals. We always enjoyed a Sunday roast and when we went to church one Sunday, just as Canon Capron was doing the sermon, I suddenly thought 'Oh no! I've forgotten to put the meat in the oven!' Eric would sit behind me in the church choir, so I whispered to him what I had done. He said 'what do you want me to do about it?' so I whispered back 'depends how much you want your Sunday roast'. He was not best pleased I can tell you but he removed himself from the choir and walked past the congregation who all thought he needed the Gents toilet. He returned just as the sermon finished and put his choir robe back on, I could hear him muttering as we sang the next hymn.

Chapter 17

NORMAL LIFE RESUMES

Another year on and we noticed the dog was ailing. We both knew it was time for him to leave us, Eric was devastated and for the only time in our married life he went to bed and locked himself away. Without going into detail nine months later our daughter was born!

I was very lucky both times having no problems bearing children. After being pregnant for nine months and feeling fine, the day came when from nowhere I didn't feel well on one Sunday afternoon. This was at 2.45pm I just didn't want anything to eat. Eric in his wisdom said I should ring the nurse. At 3.10pm I was on my way to Tiddington nursing home. I can tell you now as we approached Red Hill, the road leading to the nursing home, it was not pleasant. All I am saying is I could not sit on the car seat at all comfortably! At 3.40pm our daughter Charlotte was born. I well remember Nick, our son, visiting the next day, throwing the hospital doors wide open and shouting 'I've come to see my little sister!' Such a new and exciting time for him.

How true it is that you never get two the same! Charlotte our second child, even at a young age, seemed a different child altogether. So different that typical of girls she was not going to miss out on anything. I knew when it was my son's third birthday, I would have to keep an eye on her as she would take over the party. It was so hard keeping her at arm's length that in the end, although not walking yet, she ended up sat with Nick's friends passing the parcel! Until their late teens they had not got time for each other, but now they respect each other, but I hear this so many times from other families. Nick was quick enough to get his sister into trouble, but just as quick to help her when she needed it.

Chapter 18

TIME MOVES ON TO BLOOMING FLOWERS

I was aware of various different organisations in Alcester and as a family we always supported them. As the children grew older I was able to go back to work and in my spare time, I had thought to try and tidy the grassed area to the entrance of the road where I lived. I think I looked in despair as my friend and neighbour Jean came and chatted to me. We decided the grass needed an army but given time the two of us could reduce it to a level to admire, not as it was, touching the calves of our legs. Jean in her wisdom said she had two fly mowers in her garage so we set to and within a week it looked good enough to sit and have a picnic on. During the autumn months Jean's husband obtained a large bag of daffodil bulbs so we planted them in the grass and to this day they appear every year. Likewise, during the summer we felt a few flowers would look nice. An old willow tree had been dug out by the council as its roots were causing a problem with the drains. This left a massive hole so we cycled up to the new bypass and asked the workmen if they would consider bringing us a part of the cement pipes so we could plant it up. This they did, all for a pack of beer.

Sadly, soon after, Jean's husband passed away. Not long after she came into the shop where I worked and said she had been invited to a coffee morning and should she go? I immediately said 'yes, you must go it will do you good'. Apparently, she went and came back to the shop saying she had been asked to join something called Alcester in Bloom. She mentioned she would only join if I went with her! I had never heard of it but agreed, yes, we could go to the next meeting together.

This we did and to cut a long story short, we found lots of areas that could be changed or enhanced that we had not really noticed before. Within

Digger laying cement stone planter.

twelve months I was made Chairman. What was that all about? At this
time, I was suffering dreadful panic attacks and only telling my friend Jean.
The best advise she gave me was, even though you feel you're going to pass
out, you never will and to go along with it. How true those words were,
especially when I refused medication.

However, it did not help the situation when I was appointed the job of
Chairman and didn't know the first thing about flowers. It came to the
annual General Meeting and I had planned who to vote for as a new
Chairman. What a shock when I realised the committee had decided
behind my back it would be me. It was one of the worst panic attacks I ever
had. Jean sat next to me smiling while I so desperately whispered to her
'please Jean, you are my friend, tell them I can't do it'. No way was she
listening! All she said was 'I bet the pain in your chest feels like a brick and
your heart's beating so fast you think you will collapse? TOUGH'.

There was nothing I could do about it. I went home and told Eric who advised me to do what I thought or imagined the town would like. With permission from the District Council we started to improve the look of the town. The then island known as the Globe Island never had any flowers on so we decided to plant daffodils in the centre and polyanthus plants all around. A beautiful sight but we were then told by the District Council the island did not belong to us and to leave it alone! Our first mistake.

It wasn't long before I encouraged Eric to join the committee. What a great asset he was, there were wonderful members all willing to do hard work, not just planting, but there were times when the heavy work needed a man. John and Pauline Gilbey joined us and within months the whole committee managed to turn the town around. We introduced wooden planters, which Eric and John Gilbey made, and committee members dug out areas for planting flowers, opened up the dismal area outside the Police Station and most of all raised funds to erect 20 poles for hanging baskets in

Flowers outside the Police Station in Priory Road, Alcester.

the High Street. We began with one basket, then a few years later two hanging baskets and now in 2020 we have three hanging baskets on each pole and extended through to another street. As the local people know we constantly raise funds for the hanging baskets by requests to sponsor them. Money is raised to pay for planters, repair work, maintenance and bedding out areas. I wrote to all I could think of on the Industrial Estate, local shops, offices, churches, pubs and had a magnificent response.

Following this we entered the Heart of England In Bloom Competition. This we found increasingly hard over the years as new rules came along. We were out early in the mornings until late evenings cleaning out gutters, picking up litter, cigarette ends, weeding and watering. Each year we had just one day to show the judges around and highlight our town. The judges would arrive to the sound of the church bells, civic dignitaries were invited and then the day began.

Although everything was organised, I was not prepared for what the local community had got together for when we left the Town Hall to walk and meet everyone. The theme we thought of was V.E. Day. As we turned the corner there were the male voice choir singing old time songs, I could not speak I was so emotional! We walked onto the Church Green where all the little children were sat around the War Memorial dressed as evacuees and waving their flags. The Alcester Ladies Choir, with piano, sang and everyone just joined in the singing. I was overwhelmed. What a day that was!

I well remember one judging day when I came home and found I had lost an earring. I mentioned it to Eric to which he promptly replied 'it's probably in the judge's top pocket, you were sat close enough to him in the car'! That was Eric! However, after winning Gold for several years we eventually won the National Competition for Alcester. This was traumatic for me as I was still suffering from panic attacks. However, how could I let the committee down?

Putting everything to the back of my mind we boarded the train to Durham. I could see the three others who came with me were tense wondering what I would do. However, once on the train I was fine and just

Durham Castle and Durham Cathedral.

knew I had to see the event through. We stayed in small board and lodgings overlooking the wonderful Cathedral with cobblestones everywhere in this wonderful place.

We were up at dawn with instructions on where to go and at what time. We decided beforehand to visit the wonderful Cathedral and were able to listen to the choir rehearsing, it was a mighty steep walk but we made it. On arriving to the Great Hall, we were piped in by a lady on her bagpipes at Durham Castle. We were seated at the back, in front of the lovely Irish people we had met the night before, they were also contestants and we got on very well with them. It was a bit of a shock when we also saw them in the Cathedral with one gent wearing a chain round his neck. We waited patiently to see the nominations on the big screen and then came the overall National Winner. As the name of the winner appeared on the screen, I clapped along with everyone else and said to my fellow friends 'Leicester! I didn't know they were in the competition'. But then I realised there were

Alcester wins the Heart of England In Bloom Competition.

tears in Jean's, Eric's and John's eyes! Eric said 'Look again'. I cannot tell you the emotion that ran through me when I saw it really said Alcester!

I can remember the gentleman on the stage saying it would take me as long to walk to him as it did to get there on the train. It was all such a dream. We were all invited back somewhere for refreshment. So much was the shock and excitement that Jean went to find a telephone, as mobiles were not about then, to phone home. We could not get to the food (but were very thankful afterwards when we found out that a lot of people went down with food poisoning!).

When it was time to get on the train home we purchased sandwiches from one of the shops to eat on the way back. The atmosphere in the train was unbelievable. Everyone swapping conversations and enjoying sharing food and drink! All of a sudden a voice came over the tannoy 'would Mrs Margaret Payne please come to the front of the train for a telephone message'. Well I can tell you now I should not have had that drink! I eventually found the front of the train where I was told there was a reception waiting at Alcester Town Hall for when we got back. I was shocked! Word had soon got around our little town. As I got back to my seat I remember saying 'put the drink away there is a reception waiting for us at the Town Hall'. We were all absolutely shattered since being up from five in the morning but what a day this was turning out to be!

As we climbed the stairs of the Town Hall a deluge of people were waiting. I wanted to cry. What had happened? We had set the pace for all the other In Bloom organisations. Alcester had won the National Award! I was so overwhelmed I had to ask Jean to read out what the judges had said.

The following year we were inundated with people visiting, asking for advice, telephoning, it was a pleasure to meet so many people. I will just mention a group of people who arrived in a mini bus when Eric was busy decorating. I invited all twelve in and they showed me a very derelict place somewhere in Birmingham, when I saw the photos I thought to myself, they need an army to clear this area out. However, on judging day up came their photos on the screen, what a difference! It was now a most beautiful area which the community as a whole had taken over and not just a garden, it was more or less the size of a park. So, you see anything is possible!

News had travelled far and wide. A gentleman from up north wrote and said he was very much interested to see how we did things in Alcester. He came to visit and we walked round and I described how everyone got involved and then stopped in the local old-fashioned tearoom where we discussed how he could get things moving in his village. I saw his photos later which were like looking at a cover on a chocolate box.

Another gentleman, this time from the Royal British Legion, happened to be visiting the area and staying in the local Hotel. We met up and the conversation moved to what I did for the community. He was most impressed with all the activity that occurred and promised to return. This he has done on a few occasions when visiting the Midlands.

It is very gratifying to see the many tourists now taking a great interest in all Alcester has to offer. It was and is a very rewarding job but what tales we could tell! One very kind gentleman said instead of us constantly carrying water from the usual destination we could use his back garden where he had a tap. This was a lovely suggestion until on walking into his back garden one evening, one of our members found him reclining on his sunbed, naked! It was his private property after all so the committee member decided to leave him to relax!

The committee were and still are a Godsend to Alcester. Occasionally, when giving a gentle reminder that watering must be regular especially on hot days, for some reason especially the gents would just reply to my messages with a 'Yes Ma'am'. Do I sound that bossy?

On many occasions we held charity shops to fund raise. How lovely was that! Music going, customers singing and dancing. You don't get that every day. It was in the time when we could sell absolutely anything, certainly not junk. I well remember one couple setting up home were absolutely thrilled to buy all their bedroom furniture and other things for bargains. In some empty shops we used toilet facilities were a no no, but the shops surrounding us were very kind in allowing us to use theirs. Cakes and coffee arrived from the local bakers, we were treated as the new local staff to Alcester.

Chapter 19

INTERNET CHAT

Now you may think this odd but here we go! My life now is on the internet. We all know that some people on the internet can be very undesirable and my first word of warning to anyone interested is don't be afraid to delete! The second word of warning is NEVER giving your full name or address. But you can chat to some lovely people from all over the world and never actually meet them.

I did get lucky some years ago with a group of people in a private chatroom. I shared many conversations with Eric who at the time never used the internet. One day, someone suggested we all meet up in the Midlands. This was something I had never dreamed of! However, there were eighteen of us altogether: one lady from America, another from Scotland, one from Durham, one from Geordie land, one from Derby, a lovely couple from Essex and yes one from Holland. The rest came from the Midlands. These weekends away with such lovely people were so much fun. A couple turned up on a motorbike, I couldn't wait to whizz round on it as a pillion.

The gent from Essex was nothing but a laugh a minute. Going for breakfast one morning, there he was ready to slide down the bannister! We would visit places of interest wherever we decided to stay. I must admit the one I was looking forward to Loughborough Bell Foundry was the worst! I'm sure the person in charge was showing off as he clanged every bell imaginable and why did he lock the door after us? Either way, it was so loud we went out and left a few in there who could stand the noise.

I did enjoy Foxton Locks. The weekend was sunny and ideal for investigating. I believe they were renovating around it but it was a joy to just sit and relax with a G&T watching the different boats go by. A large pub was to hand to have a lovely lunch, an ideal place for peace and quiet.

Strangely enough, although I don't like water, the friends wanted to go to Stratford upon Avon a few miles away from us. Again, we had a lovely time. My friends knew I dreaded getting on the boat, but what can you do? I didn't end up in the water and had a really good time. This time we stayed at The Kings Court Hotel in Alcester, I can thoroughly recommend it. Yes, it was only up the road from where I live but why spoil the party?

This went on for about twelve years, meeting up twice a year but then sadly one turned out not what we thought and it all ended.

Chapter 20

FAMILY HOLIDAYS

Before the children came along, our usual holiday venue was Bournemouth. Then we missed about five years, truth was we couldn't afford it! Afterwards we decided to go to Weymouth but surprise, surprise, our favourite place was Weston-super-Mare and the surrounding area. Forget the sea! At the time they had opened a large outdoor swimming pool with attendants and all amenities. This was ideal for us all.

During this time, we had met a new church organist, he had been there awhile but somehow got attached to us as a family. It came to the summer holidays and he enquired where we would be staying, to which we replied it was going to be a caravan holiday just outside Weston-super-Mare. We explained the beach was rubbish but it was lovely for walks and that we usually went out for the day.

We arrived early Saturday morning and settled ourselves in. Come Sunday morning we decided to go for a morning walk along the back wash of Weston. The sun was shining gloriously but just as we got to the beach, the heavens opened! Thunder, lightning, hail stones and nowhere to shelter, we ran back to the caravan but it was too late, we were all soaked to the skin. Both Nick and Charlotte went to their bedrooms to change as did Eric and myself. I stripped off to barely nothing and put the gas fire on to warm us up. There I was squatting in front of the fire trying to dry out when the caravan door opened and all we could see was a large suitcase and someone shouted 'room for one more?' It was Richard the church organist! How on earth he found us we would never know.

The rest of the week was nothing but bright sunshine. Richard stayed the week, what a blessing he was! On the Tuesday, Eric had to go back home

Charlotte, Nick and Richard.

to an important meeting, leaving the four of us to fend for ourselves. I was trying to keep it quiet that I had the worst headache in a long time. Richard noticed and insisted he took me back to the caravan and he would look after Nick and Charlotte and return early evening. It made sense as by this time I was feeling quite ill. I knew if I slept it off, I would be fine and not spoil the day for others. Early evening came, I had woken up, Eric arrived back and wondered where the rest were. On saying that, in they all came having had a wonderful time. Richard left at the end of the week while we stayed on, but as he left he said 'thank you, this has been the most enjoyable week' and he had felt part of the family. Strangely in time he did become part of the family when he married our dear friend Jan. He was an extremely talented man musically and would often fit in two concerts in one night, returning to our house and collapsing in the chair.

Chapter 21

ERIC THE COUNCILLOR

It wasn't long before Eric was asked to join the Town Council, he was quite shocked and had never thought of it, he was quiet that week and I knew he was considering it. He never did anything impulsively. After much thought he agreed but retired from his every day job, saying he would devote his time now properly to the town. His motto was never jump in at Council meetings, listen to what people say for the first few weeks, feel the ground, see who did what for the community. It didn't take long before he was actively involved and especially sorting out problems for the community. It was what he had wanted to do all his life, he could be seen about town every day sorting problems out.

Flooding in Alcester was very bad in June some years ago. The first thing he, along with Sue Adams another Councillor, thought of was moving the elderly from the Malt Mill Lane Complex. What a night that was. Surprisingly enough the elderly residents did not panic and did not mind being moved to the local Town Hall where coffee, tea and biscuits were waiting for them plus made up beds. I had the pleasure of meeting one lady who thought it hilarious being bumped over the cobblestones in her wheelchair. We laughed until we cried! Who said the elderly are down spirited?

On the down side the river was rising rapidly and was well over the arches. People were stood on the bridge and ignoring the hazards, Eric went on the bridge to try and coax them off. They weren't listening. I was getting more worried that Eric, along with the others, was going to end up in the river as the bridge was bouncing. In the end the policeman on duty came and moved them off. It was to be our small town's judging day for

Alcester in Bloom two days later and I was giving up in despair thinking there was no point in the judges coming as the place was in such a mess. The shops and pubs were all flooded out, I can't tell you the assortment that was floating down the High Street.

What happened the next day? We went into town to see where to start clearing up. I have never seen so many people out with skips (where did they get those from?), shovels, spades and brooms, all working so hard to get the town right. Many knew the following day could be disastrous for the judging. However, they toiled on as best they could.

When the judges arrived I didn't have to explain anything to them. They could see the effort that the community had made in clearing up and were most understanding. Every corner we turned residents were waving and greeting the judges which delighted them. Thankfully Eric, along with Sue Adams and Mike Gittus, found a way of hopefully stopping this happen again by having a flood defence built.

On one occasion, Eric had a phone call from a lady who was moving house and asked if he, along with Sue Adams, could help clear her house out! She also mentioned her carpet was covered in ants! It was clear to see when they reached the lady's house the next day, the poor soul had dementia and there were no ants on the carpet. Suffice to say if they found tied-up carrier bags they always asked first before opening. Good job they did, some contained the ashes of the lady's deceased pets! They then ventured upstairs only to find loads and loads of knickers, the said lady said she had a fetish for buying them!

Eric fitted his duties in with bellringing, many church services, church gardening, plus his own family life. He enjoyed every minute of his official work. Our conservatory soon became an office and it became normal life to see him bob in and out to grab coffee or check any emails that had come through, then dash off out again.

We were invited to the opening of a local Coffee Shop one evening. The tables were beautifully adorned with lit candles. The guests were all very pleasant, refreshment came round and everyone was busy chatting. All of a sudden, I could smell smoke! The smell was right by me, yes Eric's coat had caught fire. He had been standing too close to the table. That was interesting following him around so as not to look as if he had picked the coat up from the local tip!

A few years later he was asked to be Mayor. We were both shocked but again it was a new experience along the way. We met twelve other Mayors from around the District, attending many functions with them in the week and during weekends. I was very wary about meeting these people as I assumed, like many others, that people with chains on had an 'air' about them. Although Eric was Mayor twice over the years, I have to say the first group were really, really nice people. No airs and graces, just normal very nice people but always doing their bit for their own community. The second time round, yes, again, all lovely people but more reserved.

Eric, after a while was invited to join the District Council. As you can imagine they were a very varied number! However Eric seemed to get on with them all individually. He had great respect for the Leader, Chris Saint as he said 'Chris knows and understands Alcester through and through, every building and every plot of land. I, personally, will be ever grateful for his help and advice on Alcester in Bloom.'

We were very privileged to go to so many events, although most invites were free, we always paid our way in donations from our own money. Holidays went out of the window.

Then another great surprise. Eric returned home, this time very fidgety! He had been asked to be Chairman of the District. This was a different kettle of fish! Far more events and appointments to go to but I knew deep down he just wanted me to say 'Go for it'. Who was I to dampen his spirits?

Yes, you are treated like royalty, but trust me we never abused it, I hope we were still the same people, not only representing our own town but also the District. We both always remembered whatever title you get it should not change you as a person, no point in putting on airs and graces, it would never last the duration of the job. All you can do is be yourself, do your best, enjoy the experience and when it's all over you are back to normal life. But it certainly was an eye opener!

We would never go into a shop wearing chains. Far to ostentatious. If we needed a pint of milk or a loaf of bread, the chains came off in the car. There were many serious events, many fun events and many educational events that we would not have missed for the world. From small villages to large towns, everyone had something to offer and to be proud of.

That particular year we devoted our life to Eric being Chairman of the District as he took this job most seriously. There are only 365 days in the year, but somehow we seemed to fit in nearly 500 attending three events in one day many times. Unlike some, we used our own car to go to local functions unless it was further out of town when a chauffeur would take us, often taking any other dignitary from Alcester.

Over the years we got to know all twelve of the chauffeurs and got on extremely well with them. When it was Eric's turn to hold a Civic Dinner, often the chauffeurs would be sat away eating a sandwich. We decided they deserved more than that so treated them to a meal at The Kings Court. We were well looked after by them, especially when dashing from one event to another knowing we had to be at a certain church on time sometimes we just got there within minutes. We would hear the chauffeurs saying, here they are, let's sort them out. One time one was running to the church door from the Car Park, one was putting my hat on straight, another had a cloth to clean my shoes and Eric was being wiped down by another as it was pouring with rain, then he said, walk in calmly as if you have been here ages. This we did. The very nice vicar greeted us and of course we shook hands and said politely how lovely it was to be there!

Often I would go straight from work after a quick brush up in the shop facilities and I would get changed in the car as we were driving to one or other destination. As I am not partial to wine, one of my friends (we will just call her Carol!) was always waiting with a G&T in the background at local functions, saying 'your mineral water madam'. God bless her, she always looked after not only me but so many people over the years. Exhausting yes, rewarding yes, but when it all stops it takes you quite a while to adjust to normality again.

Without wishing to sound morbid Eric passed away in 2018 and I would like to say a quick but very important thank you to Yvonne Hine, Di Gittus, Sue Adams and Ashley Hawkes who were there when I needed them most. They did not ask, they told me they were only too pleased just to be there.

Thank goodness for photos! I now have 10 albums of the wonderful times we had and to look back on. The many family events in more albums. Eric gave his last talk on his life, although he was not well that evening. After two hours of him and the audience laughing 'the way he told it', I thought to stand at the back and signal to him to stop. What did he do? Only announced what I was doing but then said 'ignore her, shall we carry on?' To which they all said yes. I smile now as Eric would always do what he wanted. We both had no regrets from the time we met all those years ago. Never offensive or rude or jealous Eric did his thing, I did mine, but somewhere along the line we came together. He was born to serve and that's what he did, always with a smile.

The tales recounted have certainly been part of life's rich tapestry. I think I grew with dignity after my varied early days, but I'm still the local Alcester girl who can change her hat at any time.

Maggie and Eric.

By the Same Author

Alcester: My Early Years
Maggie Payne, ISBN 978-1-85858-574-1   £7.95

Other Books on Alcester

Alcester National Schools: 1871-1903
Karyl Rees, ISBN 978-1-85858-516-1   £8.95

Alcester Victoria Silver Band – The First Hundred Years
Ed. Nigel Kift, ISBN 978-1-85858-188-0   £7.95

A Hundred Years of Alcester
Ed. John Bunting & Jean Whittington, ISBN 978-1-85858-156-9   £9.95

The Fiery Canon – The Ramblings of a Rustic Rector
David Capron, ISBN 978-1-85858-341-9   £11.95

The Puffing Parson – Branch Line Ministry
David Capron, ISBN 978-1-85858-350-1   £11.95

Transcripts of the Papers of Fulke Greville
Pauline Sands, ISBN 978-1-85858-544-4   £14.95

All the titles above are available to purchase now at:
www.brewinbooks.com